★ IT'S MY STATE! ★

Indiana

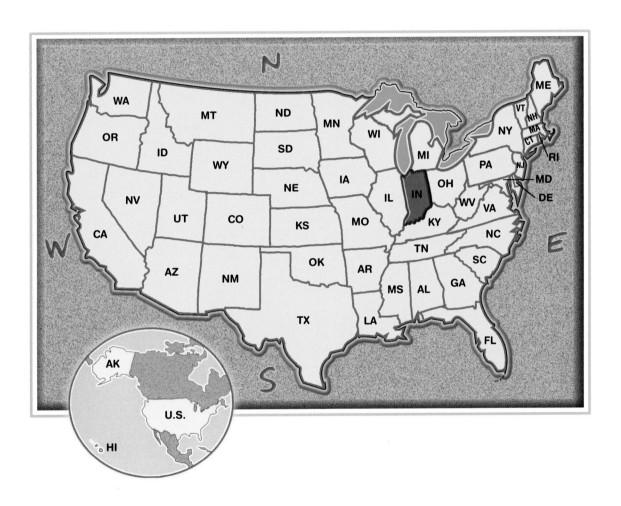

Kathleen Derzipilski

 **Marshall Cavendish**
Benchmark
New York

Marshall Cavendish Benchmark
99 White Plains Road
Tarrytown, New York 10591-9001
www.marshallcavendish.us

Library of Congress Cataloging-in-Publication Data
Derzipilski, Kathleen.
Indiana / by Kathleen Derzipilski.
p. cm. — (Its my state!)
Summary: "Surveys the history, geography, economy, and people of Indiana"—Provided by publisher.
Includes bibliographical references and index.
ISBN 0-7614-1927-6
1. Indiana—Juvenile literature. I. Title. II. Series.
F526.3.D47 2006
977.2—dc22

2005021609

Photo research by Candlepants, Inc.

Cover photo: Image Source / Picture Quest

Back cover illustration: The license plate shows Indiana's postal abbreviation, followed by its year of statehood.

The photographs in this book are used by permission and through the courtesy of: *Corbis:* Hal Horwitz, 4 (top); Reuters, 5 (top);
Historical Picture Archive , 5 (middle); Layne Kennedy, 8, 9; Alen MacWeeney, 11; Gary W. Carter, 16, 20, 33; Bettmann, 36, 39
(bottom), 48 (top), 48 (bottom), 49; David Turnley, 44; Patrick Bennett, 45, 64; Time Mosenfelder, 50; Stave Raymer, 51;
William Manning, 52; Wally McNamee, 53; Michael S. Yamashita, 66 (middle); Ralf-Finn Hestoft, 67 (bottom), 68; Roger
Ressmeyer, 69; Joseph Sohm / ChromoSohm, Inc., 71; Charles E. Rotkin, 71. *Animals Animals:* Richard Shiell, 4 (middle); Tom
Edwards, 38. *Photo Researchers, Inc.:* Stephen J. Krasemann, 4 (bottom); Will & Deni McIntyre, 5 (bottom); Michael Hubrich, 10;
A.H. Rider, 17; John Shaw, 18 (middle); Millard H. Sharp, 18 (bottom); Micahel P. Gadomski, 19 (top); Scott Camazine, 67 (top).
Airphoto: Jim Wark, 12. *Super Stock:* Richard Cummins, 13, 55; ThinkStock, 37; age fotostock, 40, 42, 43, 50, 66 (bottom), 67
(middle). *Peter Arnold, Inc.:* John ER MacGregor, 18 (top); Ed Reschke 19 (middle), 19 (bottom); Manfred Danegger, 15. *James
P. Rowan:* 21. *North Wind Picture Archive:* 24, 25, 26, 39 (top). *Indiana Historical Society:* 34, 48 (middle). *The Image Works:*
Eastcott-Momatiuk, 46; Andre Jeny, 54. *Indiana University Northwest:* 49. *Gibson Stock Photography:* Mark Gibson, 62, 73.
Envision: Andre Baranowski, 65; George Mattei, 66 (top).

Series design by Anahid Hamparian
Printed in Malaysia

1   3   5   6   4   2

Contents

A Quick Look at Indiana

Nickname: The Hoosier State
Population: 6,271,973 (2005 estimate)
Statehood: December 11, 1816

Tree: Tulip Tree

The tulip tree is the tallest tree in Indiana's forests. The tree has clusters of yellow-green, bell-shaped flowers. The distinctive leaves of the tulip tree appear on the Indiana state seal. The tulip tree is also called the yellow poplar.

Flower: Peony

The peony was chosen as the state flower in 1957. In the spring, the plants produce large, fragrant flowers in shades of white and pink. Because of their beautiful flowers and dark green, glossy leaves, peonies are grown in gardens and yards throughout Indiana.

Bird: Cardinal

The cardinal can be found in Indiana throughout the year. The male cardinal is easily identified by its bright red feathers and crest (the feathers that form a point at the top of its head). The female has brown feathers and a light red head and crest. Cardinals flit through shrubs, thickets, and trees. They eat a variety of insects, seeds, and small fruits.

Stone: Salem Limestone

Indiana limestone was formed more than 300 million years ago when the Midwest was under an inland sea. The limestone is made of layers of microscopic fossils of the animals that once lived in that sea. The beautiful, fine-textured stone is taken from quarries in central and southern Indiana. Indiana limestone has been used in many buildings throughout the country, including structures in Washington, D.C.

River: Wabash River

The Wabash River and its valley have long attracted settlers and explorers. Many Native American towns and camps were located along the Wabash. The French established trading posts and forts on the riverbanks. For early residents, the Wabash was a trade route for farm produce and other goods. The river's name comes from the Native American word, Wah-Ba-Shi-Ki, which means "pure white."

Language: English

Indiana adopted English as the official language of the state in 1984. In Indiana—as in all the other states—official meetings and business are conducted in English, and official records and legal documents are written in English. In 1995, Indiana officially recognized another language. American Sign Language (ASL) was accepted as a "standard, independent language."

1 The Hoosier State

Indiana is located in the north-central part of the United States. Roughly rectangular in shape, Indiana is bound on the south by the Ohio River. Its northwest corner touches Lake Michigan, one of the Great Lakes. Indiana has an area of 36,291 square miles. In size, it is the thirty-eighth largest state.

Land Shaped by Glaciers and an Ancient Sea

About 300 million years ago, North America was under water. Over the last one million years, the continent has experienced several Ice Ages. Glaciers—large, slow-moving ice masses—have repeatedly formed and traveled over the land. As the glaciers moved, they shaped the land. Then, as the climate warmed, these masses of ice melted and retreated northward. Scientists estimate that the land that now includes Indiana has been under glaciers eleven times in the last million years. Proof of the ancient sea and the glaciers is visible in the geography of Indiana.

Indiana's Borders
North: Michigan
South: Kentucky
East: Ohio
West: Illinois

7

The movement of the glaciers left most of Indiana flat or rolling and covered with sandy, fertile soil called till. The pockets of marshes and ponds in the northern part of the state are another sign of the thawing glaciers. The glaciers carved up the land and left water behind. The sand dunes along the shores of Lake Michigan are the windblown debris or remnants of past glaciers. As each glacier formed and then melted, it reshaped the region's rivers and the shoreline of Lake Michigan.

Southern Indiana was largely untouched by the glaciers, but it was affected by the great inland sea. While the land was under the water, layers of limestone and dolomite—a type of mineral—were laid down. These stones were easily dissolved and eroded by underground streams. The result is the hilly surface and the knobs, ravines, bluffs, and sinkholes found in

Tufts of grass dot the sand dunes at the Indiana Dunes National Lakeshore along Lake Michigan.

Many of Indiana's underground caves have interesting mineral formations. Visitors to Indiana can view these at sites such as Marengo Cave.

southern Indiana. Streams disappear into the ground or emerge as springs. Many caves can be found underground. This type of landscape is called karst.

Forests and Prairies

Most of Indiana's trees are deciduous hardwoods such as maple, elm, ash, beech, hickory, oak, cherry, walnut, and yellow poplar. In the autumn, the leaves of deciduous trees change color and fall from the branches. Trees that require the same kind of soil and moisture grow side-by-side in the same forest.

In the fall, Indiana's forests are a mix of orange, yellow, green, and red as the leaves change for the season.

Softwood trees such as cypress and cottonwood grow in some of the wetlands.

Forests originally covered about 85 percent of Indiana. However, by 1922, the forests were so extensively cut that the state forester predicted that Indiana would one day have no forests at all. But that prediction proved to be wrong. Instead, over the last century, the number of acres with trees has increased. Today about 20 percent of the state has forests. Most of the trees are in the southern half of the state. William Hoover, a professor at Purdue University, sees the re-growth of the forests as "a tribute to the resiliency of nature."

People enjoy the beauty and seasonal changes of Indiana's forests. For many animals, birds, and insects, the trees are needed for their survival. The forests are their habitat. Trees also help to clean the air and to prevent soil erosion, (If too much soil erodes or wears away the nutrients in the soil would be lost, and plants and trees would not be able to grow roots and survive.) Trees are also valued as a building material.

The tallgrass prairie of the central United States and Canada extends into northwest Indiana. At one time, prairies covered about 15 percent of Indiana. The prairie has marshy areas as well as sparse stands of shrubs and oaks. Fire is necessary to the life cycle of the prairie. Fire keeps the prairie open (with few or no trees) so grasses and wildflowers can have all the sunlight they need. Grasses and prairie plants survive the fires because they have deep, widespread roots. Even if the top of the plants are burned, the roots are safe and able to send up new green growth after the fire has been put out.

Most of Indiana's prairie and wetlands have been lost to development of farms, roads, buildings, and other structures. But the soils, of course, remain and are now the base of some of Indiana's richest farmland.

Much of Indiana's natural prairies was used for agricultural products, such as wheat.

Rivers and Water

Indiana has two watersheds. (A watershed is a large area that is drained by rivers and other bodies of water.) One of the state's watersheds occupies a narrow strip across northern Indiana. Here, the rivers flow toward the Saint Lawrence River, which continues to the Atlantic Ocean. The rivers of the other watershed flow toward the Ohio River and then on to the Mississippi River and into the Gulf of Mexico. The rise of land separating the two watersheds is called the Valparaiso moraine. It is a ridge of rubble left by one of the glaciers.

The Wabash River is the major river of Indiana. It rises in Ohio, flows west across Indiana, and then turns south. It forms the southern half of Indiana's western boundary and becomes increasingly twisty. The Wabash meets the Ohio River at the southwest corner of Indiana. Tributaries of the Wabash include

The Wabash and Ohio rivers meet along the Indiana-Illinois border. The rivers provide needed moisture to the surrounding fertile land.

Sugar Creek and the Mississinewa, Tippecanoe, and Eel Rivers in the north and the Patoka and White Rivers in the south. The White River has two long forks. The Kankakee River crosses northwest Indiana; and the Whitewater River, near the eastern boundary, flows toward the Ohio River. In southern Indiana, sand dunes edge sections of the Wabash and White Rivers.

The Saint Marys and the Saint Joseph rivers drain northeastern Indiana. They meet to form the Maumee River. The Maumee empties into Lake Erie. The city of Fort Wayne grew at this junction of the three rivers.

The city of South Bend was founded along the Saint Joseph River.

The Grand Calumet and the Little Calumet are two slow-moving rivers that empty into Lake Michigan. The industrial area in the northwest corner of Indiana is named the Calumet Region after these two rivers.

Indiana's water supply is drawn from the ground water and from rivers and streams. Individuals, farms, industries, and state agencies work together to keep the water supply free of contamination.

The Seasons

Indiana has four distinct seasons. Winters are cold, with an average temperature near freezing. Snowstorms and ice are common, with the north of the state receiving more snow than the south. In spring, the days become longer and warmer. Summers are hot and humid. Day after day, the daytime temperature can stay in the 90s. In the fall, the days grow shorter and cooler.

Indiana receives about 40 inches of precipitation each year. Most of this is in the form of rain. Thunderstorms can travel through Indiana and, occasionally, destructive tornadoes touch down.

Wildlife

Some of the mammals living in Indiana include moles, shrews, chipmunks, squirrels, bats, woodchucks, and opossums. The beaver, once hunted for its fur, builds its lodges in the state's ponds and streams. Foxes and bobcats are sometimes seen. Deer are so numerous that in some state parks, they have eaten most of the vegetation. To keep the deer population in check, hunters with bows and arrows are allowed to take a limited number of the animals.

Young foxes—called fox kits—wait for their mother outside their burrow.

Fish such as bass, catfish, pike, and sunfish are plentiful in the lakes and streams. They provide food for wild animals, but also make fishing popular in the state's bodies of water. Darters—a kind of small fish that lives in streams—and eyeless cave fish are rare and are not fished for sport.

Many birds pass through Indiana on their spring and fall migrations. Other birds are year-round residents. Ducks, geese, herons, and bitterns frequent the marshes and ponds. Meadowlarks, sparrows, warblers, orioles, wrens, blue jays, thrushes, woodpeckers, and flickers are common on the edges of fields and in wooded areas. Birds of prey, such as owls, hawks, and peregrine falcons, hunt small animals and other birds. Osprey and bald eagles are rare, though wildlife experts are working to increase these large birds' numbers.

Patient fishermen wait for their catch in the early morning fog in the Muscatatuck National Wildlife Reserve in Seymour.

Indiana

Endangered Species in Indiana

Habitat loss is the main reason that plants and animals become rare or extinct. In Indiana, the landscape has changed greatly since pioneer days. As a result, certain species are extinct or endangered. In other instances, some species only survive in small areas.

The karner blue butterfly is one of the endangered species of Indiana. The wings of the small and pretty butterfly are blue on top. The gray undersides have orange and black spots. The karner blue lives in northern Indiana in grassy areas that have a scattering of oak trees. In summer, this butterfly flutters among the wildflowers in the open sunny patches. The females lay eggs on wild lupine, the only plant the caterpillars of this species eat.

People are working to restore the natural areas used by the karner blue. They have thinned the trees in some areas to make room for the prairie plants and have planted more lupine. Specialists raise the butterflies in captivity to be sure they have lupine on which to lay their eggs and to ensure that the caterpillars have lupine to eat. Student Ali DeVries wrote, "People should be honored to have this butterfly inhabit our state."

The karner blue's striking color makes for a beautiful sight amid Indiana's green plants.

Plants & Animals

Indiana Bat

During the winter, the Indiana bat hibernates in dense clusters in caves. Only a few caves in southern Indiana are suitable for this rare bat. In spring, Indiana bats migrate to wooded areas near streams and rivers. They find places under peeling bark to roost and to raise their young. At night, they feed on flying insects.

Fox Squirrel

Fox squirrels live in forests close to Indiana's prairie or near cleared land. They dart between the trees and up and down the trunks and branches. For a nest, they weave together twigs with the leaves on them or move into an old woodpecker nest. Fox squirrels eat acorns, hickory nuts, and beechnuts and bury the extras for use later.

Robin

At sunrise, robins are among the first birds to start singing. They run over the lawns and stop to look for earthworms. As fall approaches, they comb the shrubs for berries. Most robins migrate south for the winter, but if there is enough food, some robins will stay all year in Indiana.

Hickory

There are several types of hickory trees growing throughout Indiana. Hickory trees produce hard-shelled nuts. The nuts must be buried by squirrels if they are to sprout. In autumn the leaves of the hickory turn yellow.

Big Bluestem Grass

Big bluestem grass is one of the grasses of the tallgrass prairie. The stems grow to about 6 feet high and the narrow leaves can be about 2 feet long. In late fall and winter when there is frost, the leaves turn reddish bronze.

Box Turtle

Box turtles have high-domed shells. Their shells can have different patterns or designs. When threatened, they pull their head, legs, and tail completely inside. Box turtles live on the forest floor where it is cool and damp.

2 From the Beginning

Ancient People

People have been living in the area that became the state of Indiana for at least 12,000 years. The people who lived in this area between 2000 BCE and 750 BCE are of the Archaic tradition, a term that historians and scientists have used to describe these ancient people. One sign of where they lived are huge piles of mussel shells that they left beside some of the region's streams.

The next group who inhabited the area are referred to as the people of the Woodland tradition. They lived throughout the Mississippi and Ohio valleys between 750 BCE and 900 CE. They built mounds of earth near their villages. The mounds were important in their ceremonies. Mounds State Park on the bluffs overlooking the White River has some of these mounds from the Woodland period.

People of the Mississippian tradition, who lived in the area of Indiana from 900 CE to 1650, also built mounds. Angel Mounds, a large town that was built during the Mississippian

Young boys living in Indianapolis in 1908 wait to collect newspapers to be delivered.

Sites like Angel Mounds near Evansville provide visitors with a chance to learn about ancient cultures.

period near the place where the Ohio and Wabash rivers meet, was a center for government, religion, and trade for these people. Several smaller communities from the Mississippian period were clustered along the rivers close to Angel Mounds.

Modern Native Americans

The Miami were among the Native American groups living in the 1600s across the region that includes present-day Indiana. They lived in the northern area along the Saint Joseph River and in the Wabash Valley. Their principal town, Kekionga, grew where the Saint Joseph and Saint Marys rivers meet to form the Maumee River. Two groups closely related to the Miami in language and culture were the Wea and the Piankashaw. The Delaware, Shawnee, and Potawatomi moved into Indiana in the 1700s.

Europeans

French traders and missionaries—people who brought Christianity to new areas—came to the area in the first half of the 1600s. They pressed west from Canada by way of the rivers and lakes. They were eager to discover if they could make money off the land and to meet with the native people in the area. One early explorer was La Salle. He explored Lake Michigan and the Saint Joseph and Kankakee rivers during the fall of 1679 and the winter of 1680. He continued west to the upper Mississippi River.

News that the land had abundant wildlife, especially beavers and other valuable fur-bearing animals, brought more explorers and traders to the region. Where possible, missionaries also came and settled near the Native American villages.

To have some control over the trade in the Wabash Valley, the French built three forts.

The name Indiana means "land of the Indians."

The first was built around 1720 at Ouiatenon, the principal Wea settlement. Fort Miami was built next to Kekionga in about 1722. The third fort was established at Vincennes, next to the Piankashaw, in about 1732.

During the 1700s, France and England were at war with each other. When the war ended in 1763, Canada and the land east of the Mississippi River, which included what would become Indiana, passed from France to England. That same year King George proclaimed that the land west of the Appalachian Mountains was to be reserved for Native Americans. No whites could enter or settle there, and traders needed a permit to do business in this area. Despite this law, people did cross the Appalachians to settle in the Ohio and Wabash valleys.

During the Revolutionary War, George Rogers Clark and his troops crossed the Wabash River to successfully take the fort at Vincennes from the British.

A New Nation

In the late 1770s, American colonists fought the British for their independence. After the Revolutionary War ended, the newly formed government of the United States signed the Treaty of Paris of 1783. Since the United States won the war and defeated Great Britain, the treaty gave the United States the right to all the land east of the Mississippi River. The land north of the Ohio River, called the Northwest, also was given to the United States. In 1787, Congress passed the Northwest Ordinance, which established the Northwest Territory. The state of Indiana would soon be carved from this territory.

In 1800, Congress created the Indiana Territory. William Henry Harrison was appointed as the governor of the territory. Harrison made many treaties with the Native American groups. These treaties stated that the Native Americans agreed to give

General Harrison defeated Tecumseh's warriors at the Battle of Tippecanoe. This battle was one of the losses that led to the Native Americans being forced from their native lands.

up their land. Because of the treaties, some groups had to move to reservations within the region and others had to leave the area completely. Many Native Americans moved to land west of the Mississippi River.

Tecumseh, a leader of the Shawnee people, rallied many Native Americans to oppose the white people who were settling on the traditional land of the Native Americans. His followers gathered at the junction of the Tippecanoe and Wabash Rivers.

Governor Harrison did not like the idea that the Native Americans might be preparing for war against the white people. So on November 7, 1811, Harrison led an army against the Shawnee in what would be called the Battle of Tippecanoe. Tecumseh and his men were defeated.

In 1813, in the Battle of the Thames, Native Americans were again defeated by Governor Harrison and his men. By

A settler's cabin stands in a clearing in the woods near Indianapolis in the early 1800s.

1815, most Native Americans had been forced out of the Indiana Territory.

As more white settlers came to Indiana Territory, it was divided into smaller units. Michigan Territory was created in 1805, and Illinois Territory in 1809. Then Indiana prepared to become a state. In the summer of 1816, delegates met to write a state constitution. On August 15 of that same year, Jonathan Jennings was elected governor. A few months later, on December 11, 1816, Indiana became the nineteenth state.

After Indiana became a state, more and more people moved to the area. Many of these pioneers came to the state by way of the Ohio River. They came from Kentucky, Virginia, North Carolina, Pennsylvania, and New York. Though the Indiana constitution did not permit slavery, some white settlers brought their slaves with them. Together with the few free blacks who settled in the new state, the population of African Americans also started to grow.

When Indiana Territory was created in 1800, Vincennes was the capital. In 1813, the seat of government moved to Corydon. The capital remained in Corydon when Indiana became a state in 1816. In 1820, the General Assembly decided to build a new capital, to be located at the center of the state. They chose to call this place Indianapolis. The state government moved to Indianapolis in 1825.

The land these new arrivals entered was densely wooded. It could take years for a farmer and his family to clear their land of all the trees and stumps. But once it was cleared, the land served them well. As soon as a field was clear enough to be planted, corn, hay, potatoes, and flax were the first crops to go in. Corn was a nutritious food, for both the family and their hogs. The extra corn was often made into whiskey. Fiber from the flax was woven into cloth. The trees that were cut down were used to build log cabins, fences, boats, and wagons. The wood was also burned for warmth.

One group of new settlers, the Rappites, a religious group led by George Rapp, came to Indiana in 1814. They wanted to create and to live in a harmonious, or peaceful, community. So they founded the town of Harmonie. At Harmonie, they produced everything they needed and lived comfortably in solidly built stone and wood buildings. In 1825, the town was sold to Robert Owen and William McClure. Owen planned New Harmony as a model town in which everyone would be equal and all food and other supplies would be shared. But the people in New Harmony squabbled endlessly. Owen's experiment lasted for only two years.

Making Potpourri

To keep their homes, clothes, and blankets smelling sweet, settlers used a combination of dried flowers and herbs. Potpourri, as this fragrant mixture is called, is still used today. Follow these directions to make some homemade potpourri.

What You Need

2 or 3 covered jars
Enough of the following to fill 4 or 5 cups total:
    flower petals (such as roses, violets, or hollyhocks)
    herbs (such as lavender or rosemary)
    spices (such as cinnamon sticks or cloves)
    orange or lemon peels
A spoon
Several sheets of newspaper

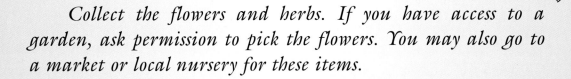

Collect the flowers and herbs. If you have access to a garden, ask permission to pick the flowers. You may also go to a market or local nursery for these items.

Spread the newspaper in a warm, dry area where the flowers and herbs will not be disturbed. Leave the flowers, herbs, and lemon or orange peel to dry out for about eight to ten days.

Once everything is dry, pick off the petals and leaves. Make separate piles for each type of flower and herb.

Allow these to dry for another eight to ten days. Check on the leaves and petals every day to make sure they are drying out evenly.

When everything is dry, try combining the materials to find the scents you like. Cinnamon or cloves, for example, will produce a spicy aroma. Flower blossoms and lavender create a sweet floral scent. Adding the orange or lemon peel to a mixture will change the scent a bit.

When you have the combination of scents, put them in separate jars. Cover the jars and let them age for about two weeks. Be sure to shake the jars at least once a day so the ingredients are mixed.

You can put the potpourri in open dishes to make a room smell nice, or put it in little pouches as gifts for your family and friends.

President Abraham Lincoln's family was among the early settlers who came from Kentucky. Abraham Lincoln was seven years old when his father took the family across the Ohio River into Indiana. The Lincolns arrived in 1816 and stayed for fourteen years before moving to Illinois. Like many other Indiana families, the Lincolns lived on a large tract of land—about 160 acres. But only a small part was cleared and farmed.

During early statehood, although most Native Americans had already left the area, a few groups still remained in Indiana. However, treaties that were negotiated with the Wea, Miami, Delaware, and Potawatomi in 1818 took away more of their land or required them to move farther west. The Potawatomi were forced to leave in 1838, and the Miami finally surrendered the last parcel of Native American land in the state in 1840.

Transportation and Internal Improvements

Transportation was of great concern to the new state. People wanted a dependable way to transport goods to markets in the eastern and southern states. To build a network of roads, canals, and railroads seemed to be the answer.

In 1828, the legislature decided on the route for a north-south highway through the state. This would be called the Michigan Road. The National Road, another road, was built to run east and west. It was used by wagons that carried people and goods from as far away as Maryland to the east and on to Illinois to the west.

In 1836, the legislature passed the Mammoth Internal Improvements Act. The act provided $13 million to be used to build canals and rail lines and to improve the roads. Unfortunately, only small sections of the canals were built at that time.

It would not be until 1852, that the Wabash-Erie Canal, which went from Lake Erie to Fort Wayne and then south to Evansville, would be completed. But by then, canals were not as useful as they might have been twenty years earlier. By the 1850s, railroads had become the preferred means of long-distance travel.

Slavery and the Civil War

Many people in Indiana thought there was nothing wrong with having slaves in the southern states or even in the new western territories and states. So they passed laws that were meant to prevent or to at least discourage free blacks (African Americans who had never been slaves or had been legally freed from slavery) from settling in Indiana. Few Indianans believed that slavery should be abolished or made illegal. Nevertheless, the Underground Railroad, which helped fugitive slaves flee to Canada, did have routes through Indiana. The journey was risky for the slaves and for their guides and protectors. The Quaker town of Fountain City was known as a station on the Underground Railroad. Many fugitives found shelter there in the home of Levi and Catharine Coffin.

People who live in Indiana are called Hoosiers. The nickname was already popular in the 1830s when it began to appear in print. Many people have tried to explain the origin of the word, but no explanation is completely convincing.

Meanwhile, in 1851, voters in Indiana approved the new state constitution. Article XIII of the constitution stated harsh rules regarding African Americans. It made it illegal for African Americans to come into or to settle in Indiana. It prohibited anyone from giving a job to an African American. In addition, any legal agreements made with African Americans would be considered worthless. In 1866, the Indiana supreme court declared Article XIII null and void, which means that they voted against it. This law was completely cancelled in 1881.

Even before the Civil War began in 1861, Indianans debated whether the Southern states should be permitted to secede or separate from the Union. Many Hoosiers sympathized with the Southern states. But Governor Oliver Morton believed that the Union should be preserved. So during the Civil War, Indiana sent men to fight on the Union (or Northern) side. There was little actual fighting in the state during the Civil War.

Leading to the Twentieth Century

By 1860, the landscape of Indiana was greatly changed from what it had been in the time of the pioneers. About one half of the forests had been cleared. Roads, railroads, and waterways made it easier for people to come to Indiana or for Indianans to visit other states.

During this time, most Hoosiers still lived on farms, but the small towns were growing. There were many new mills and factories using the resources of Indiana to manufacture a great variety of industrial and household inventions. With the end of the Civil War, immigration from the South to Indiana was renewed. The population, once concentrated in the southern half of the state, began to spread northward.

The Grange, a social and educational organization for farmers and their families, came to Indiana in 1869. Grange members joined together and formed cooperatives. This allowed them to bargain for more favorable shipping rates for their produce. The Grange also asked state legislators for better tax rates and to have mail delivered to addresses in rural areas.

Laborers in Indiana's factories became active in trade and labor unions that brought people together so they could bargain with the factory owners for better working conditions. The Knights of Labor, a group that fought for workers' rights, allowed women to be members and worked to get approval of an eight-hour workday, instead of the usual ten- or twelve-hour days that many people at that time were forced to work.

Natural gas was discovered in eastern Indiana in 1876. Ten years later, gas wells tapped the natural fuel so that it could be used. People thought the gas supply would last forever. Anyone who opened a factory could use the gas for free. This free gas

Indianans of all ages worked long hours in dangerous conditions in the state's many mills and factories.

lead to Kokomo and Anderson being transformed into manufacturing towns. Muncie, called the City of Eternal Gas, was known for glassmaking and steel, nail, and wire production. But by the turn of the century, the gas was all used up and the industrial boom fizzled out.

But progress continued in Indiana. For instance, Elwood Haynes test drove a self-propelled, gas-powered vehicle on the roads outside of Kokomo on July 4, 1894. Within a few years, Indiana had hundreds of companies building cars and making car parts. Studebaker, which had started in 1852 as a blacksmith shop and wagon-maker, began to make electric cars in 1902. Then in 1912, the company switched to making gas-powered cars. Cars changed how people spent their leisure time. "We got to go to lots of things we couldn't go to if we didn't have a

This illustration shows the Studebaker Vehicle Works in South Bend around 1908.

Indiana

car," reported an Indiana woman in the 1920s. Indiana was the center for car manufacturing until 1937, when Michigan gained the lead.

At the turn of the century, from the 1800s to the 1900s the Calumet region, east of Chicago, was developing into one of the nation's important industrial centers. The Standard Oil Company began building an enormous oil refinery at Whiting in 1889. Inland Steel started constructing a steel mill at East Chicago in 1901.

Then in 1905, United States Steel Corporation bought nine thousand acres on the shore of Lake Michigan. It had plans to level the sand dunes and to build the world's largest steel mill. It would also build a town, to be named Gary. Rail lines and harbors already served the region, and numerous large and small mills and plants opened in the Calumet. People heard there were jobs to be had at U.S. Steel Corporation and came to Indiana to work. Many of them came from as far away as eastern Europe, including Poles, Hungarians, Czechs, and Slovaks.

Things were not always positive in the early part of the twentieth century. For instance, the Ku Klux Klan (which is also referred to as the KKK) was revived in Indiana, in Evansville, in 1920. The KKK was an organization that was against African Americans and people of Jewish and Catholic faiths. Membership in the Klan grew to 300,000 people in Indiana by 1923. In the 1924 elections, the influence of the Klan helped the governor, the majority of the state legislators, and several city mayors to win office. The power of the Klan in Indiana crumbled after its leader D. C. Stephenson was convicted of murder in 1925.

Another hardship came to Indiana in the late 1920s. The Great Depression, which started in 1929, hit Indiana hard. Prices for farm products dropped and factories closed or cut back on their operations. Overall, about one quarter of the people in the state were out of work. And in some towns, unemployment was as high as 50 percent. In southern Indiana, the flooding of the Ohio River in 1937 added even more hardship.

During this time, African Americans were faced with even more challenges. Indiana had separate schools for white and black students. Segregated schools remained legal in Indiana until 1949. This often meant that African-American children attended poorer schools that were not equipped with materials

Many of Indiana's African Americans protested against the unequal standards in the state. These men are calling attention to the segregation in Indiana's public schools.

that white students had. Desegregation laws—which were designed to make things equal for African Americans and whites—went into effect, but some school districts disregarded them. It would take many more decades for some schools to arrange to have black and white students together.

Life started to get a little better around the middle of the century. During World War II, Indiana's economy bounced back. Farms and industries, especially steel, helped to supply the war effort. Then, after World War II, manufacturers turned their attention to making consumer goods. For instance, things like refrigerators were made in Evansville. So many refrigerators were made there that Evansville became known as the refrigerator capital.

During the 1950s, many people began to buy houses in the suburbs around Indiana's larger cities. Many small stores

As Indiana's cities and suburbs grew, roads, interstates, and highways were expanded and improved to accommodate larger populations.

in the downtown areas of large cities closed their doors and moved to the new shopping malls, which were often located in the suburbs. This made the downtown areas of large cities look empty and worn out. Then in the 1960s, to correct this problem, money was provided for urban renewal projects. This money helped cities like Indianapolis and Gary to benefit from the creation of new housing and business districts, as well as civic, cultural, and recreational facilities.

During the 1970s, 1980s, and 1990s, Indiana weathered a cycle of economic good times and bad times. Some businesses and industries failed while others flourished. Many people from across the country and around the world moved to the state. But, through it all, residents of the state remained strong and continued to work toward making their state the best it can be.

Hoosiers young and old are committed to preserving their beautiful state.

Important Dates

12,000 BCE Ancient people live in the region that will include present-day Indiana.

1100-1450 CE Angel Mounds is a site for early Native American communities.

1679 French explorer La Salle and his party cross Indiana.

1783 The American Revolution ends. Land that includes Indiana is given to the United States.

La Salle

1787 The Northwest Territory is created.

1800 The Indiana Territory is created.

1816 Indiana becomes the nineteenth state on December 11, 1816.

1825 The state government meets in Indianapolis, the new capital.

1836 The Mammoth Internal Improvements Act is passed to improve conditions in Indiana.

1894 Elwood Haynes test drives an early automobile.

1889 Standard Oil Company builds an oil refinery at Whiting.

1905 United States Steel Corporation builds a steel plant in the Calumet region.

1911 The Indianapolis 500 auto race begins.

1966 Indiana Dunes National Lakeshore is established.

1970 Orville Redenbacher starts his popcorn company in Indiana and calls it the Redbow Popcorn Company.

1988 Dan Quayle, a politician from Indiana, becomes vice president.

Orville Redenbacher

1990 A record of thirty-seven tornadoes tears through thirty-one Indiana counties on June 2.

2006 For the first time since 1970, most Indiana counties began observing Daylight Saving Time.

3 The People

The people of Indiana are a mix of long-time Hoosiers and new immigrants, and represent the variety of histories and heritages that have come together in Indiana. Most people in Indiana belong to families who have lived in the state for several generations. About 75 percent of Indiana's people were born in the state, and nearly everyone—97 percent—was born in the United States. If they move, Hoosiers do not move far. They tend to move within the same county they have been living in or to a county close by. Indiana has only a handful of mid-sized cities, so many Hoosiers live in small towns or in the suburbs around the bigger cities.

As the population of the United States has grown, the center of the population has moved west across the nation. But at one time, between 1890 and 1940, the center of the U.S. population was in Indiana.

The population of Indiana is concentrated in the middle and in the north of the state.

Indianapolis's downtown skyline can be seen from this viewpoint in White River State Park.

A view of Evansville at night.

Indiana

Most of Indiana's early settlers came to build and work farms on the state's fertile lands.

Marion County, in the center of the state, has the highest population. Indiana's largest city is Indianapolis, and it is the state capital. It is located in Marion County.

Lake County, in the north and east of Chicago, Illinois, is the second-largest county. Allen County, also in the north, is the third-largest county. Fort Wayne is the second-largest city of Indiana and is located in Allen County.

Evansville, in southern Indiana, is the third-largest city. Other sizable cities are South Bend, Gary, Hammond, Bloomington, Muncie, Anderson, and Terre Haute. Many of Indiana's towns have only a few hundred and sometimes a few thousand residents.

In Indiana, 88 percent of the population is white. Many

Indiana is also home to Amish communities. These girls are heading home from their school near Shipshewana.

white people trace their roots to the English, Scottish, Irish, and German settlers who came to Indiana in the 1800s. Poles, Czechs, Slovaks, Hungarians, Serbs, Croatians, Slovenes, and other eastern Europeans, as well as Greeks and Italians, came to northern Indiana in the early 1900s to work in the region's steel mills and in other industries.

African Americans make up 8 percent of the population in Indiana. Many African Americans in Indiana are descended from people who moved to the state from the South. During the first half of the 1800s, African Americans came as freemen, slaves, freed slaves, or runaway slaves. They worked at trades and as laborers and farmers. Some African Americans started all-black farming communities. Greenville Settlement, founded in 1822, Cabin Creek, founded in 1825, and Beech, founded in 1829, were among the first of

Many Indiana residents came to the state for job opportunities and Indiana's good schools.

these settlements. Many of these communities have since disappeared, but Lyles Station, which was started around 1840, still has families living there.

After the abolition of slavery in 1865, African Americans came north into Indiana so they could buy land, find work, or farm. After World War I, African Americans began again to head to Indiana in great numbers. Many went to the Calumet region to work in the industries there.

Today, the black population is greatest in Indiana's industrial counties and in the cities. The population of both Marion County and Lake County is 25 percent African American. The city of Gary is 84 percent African American.

Other races have low representation in Indiana. One percent of the population is Asian American. Most Asian Americans live in the larger cities and in the university towns

Hoosiers fill a crowded town beach at Michigan City on Lake Michigan.

of West Lafayette and Bloomington. Native Americans, Native Alaskans, Native Hawaiians, and other Pacific Islanders represent less than 1 percent of the population in Indiana.

Latinos

On the census taken every ten years, people may identify themselves as being Hispanic or Latino. They or their families are from a Spanish-speaking nation or culture. People who are Latino may be of any race. Indiana Latinos make up 4 percent of the population, a small proportion when compared to the fact that Latinos make up 13 percent of the entire United States population. The majority of Indiana's Latinos trace their roots to Mexico. Other Latinos in Indiana are from Puerto Rico and the Central American countries of Honduras and El Salvador.

> *East Chicago was a great place to grow up. It was an extremely diverse community. Roy, Lou, and I were very much aware of our Mexican roots, but we also had a strong sense of being Americans.*
> —Dr. William M. Vega, whose father worked in the steel mills of East Chicago

Many people from Mexico moved to the Calumet region of Indiana in the 1920s. Some found jobs with the railroad companies. Others worked in the steel mills there.

More recently, in the last two decades, the Latino population in Indiana has grown rapidly. One third of the foreign-born immigrants who settle in Indiana are from Mexico. Many Mexicans who come to Indiana move there to join their families and to find good jobs. Today the greatest number of Latinos lives in Lake County and Elkhart County, and in the city of Indianapolis.

Population Changes

Year by year the population of Indiana slowly increases. This increase is due to natural increases, which means that there are more births than deaths. There are still new residents coming to Indiana from other states and other countries.

Despite the increases in population, there are more people moving out of the state than are people moving into

Famous Indianans

The Lilly Family: Pharmacists and Businessmen

Eli Lilly was born in 1838 in Maryland and his family moved to Indiana in 1852. Lilly studied chemistry and the medicinal uses of plants and other substances. In 1876, Lilly opened a plant in Indianapolis to manufacture and research high-quality prescription drugs. The company grew, and in 1881 it was incorporated as Eli Lilly and Company. Later Lilly generations continued to run the company.

Gene Stratton-Porter: Writer and Naturalist

The naturalist Gene Stratton-Porter was born in Wabash County, Indiana, in 1863. In 1895, she lived near the Limberlost Swamp in northern Indiana. Stratton-Porter observed the wildlife of the swamp and photographed the birds and the moths. She wrote articles for nature magazines and illustrated them with her photographs. She also wrote stories that became best sellers.

Larry Bird: Basketball Player

Larry Bird was born in West Baden, Indiana, in 1956. He was a top-scoring player for his high school basketball team at French Lick and for his college team, Indiana State University. Bird joined the Boston Celtics in 1979 and played thirteen seasons with them. His outstanding team playing was noted with many awards. In 1992, he won a gold medal at the Olympics playing on the U.S. "Dream Team." Bird coached the Indiana Pacers from 1997 to 2003.

William Albert Wirt: School Administrator

William Albert Wirt was born in Markle, Indiana, in 1874. In 1907, he became the superintendent of schools for the new town of Gary. Wirt believed that students needed periods of work, study, and play. In Gary he designed the school buildings to have classrooms, workshops, and gymnasiums, as well as an auditorium and swimming pool. Outside, students had a park, playgrounds, and gardens where they played and worked. Instead of sitting at one desk all day, students moved from room to room and from teacher to teacher. The Gary system became famous and was adopted by many other school systems.

Janet Guthrie: Race Car Driver

Though she was not born in Indiana, Janet Guthrie made Indiana history in the 1970s. In 1977 Guthrie was the first woman to compete in the Indianapolis 500. A skilled race car driver, she also was also the first woman to race in the Daytona 500, a famous car race in Florida. Before racing at the Indy 500, Janet Guthrie had also been a pilot, a flight instructor, and an engineer.

John Mellencamp: Musician

John Mellencamp was born in 1951 in Seymour, Indiana. He plays guitar, writes songs, and sings. Mellencamp has recorded many albums, and many of his songs have made it into the Top Ten. In 1985, he and the musicians Willie Nelson and Neil Young organized Farm Aid, an annual concert to raise money for small family farms. Mellencamp lives in Bloomington.

In Indiana—as in many Midwestern states—small family farms are closed and abandoned because they cannot compete with larger farms and factories.

Indiana. The people who move away are often young and are college educated. And this is causing a problem for Indiana.

Indiana has excellent colleges and universities that prepare its students for jobs in science, high technology, business, and education. But after graduation, many of these young people find work in other states.

A number of men who became astronauts studied at Indiana's Purdue University. Among them were Neil Armstrong, the first man to walk on the moon, and Eugene Cernan, the last man to walk on the moon.

Indiana is home to many schools and their loyal sports fans. A young fan autographs the basketball hat "Captain Hoosier" is wearing for an Indiana University basketball game.

Indiana's business and education leaders worry about the effect this loss has on Indiana's economy. They are working to create research centers and companies to make Indiana attractive to these talented young people as well as to other people who may want to come live in this beautiful state.

Calendar of Events

George Rogers Clark Day

During the American Revolution, George Rogers Clark led a Kentucky militia across the Ohio River. He was determined to drive the British from the region so Americans could safely settle and trade there. In Indiana, George Rogers Clark Day is observed on February 25, the day in 1779 when the British surrendered the fort at Vincennes to Clark.

March Madness

Hoosiers have a passion for high school basketball. Competition among the boys' and girls' high school teams begins in November. In March, the teams with the most wins go to Indianapolis to play in the finals tournaments. The winners of the finals are the state champions.

Indianapolis 500

In the Indianapolis 500, thirty-three cars race two hundred times around the Speedway to cover a total distance of 500 miles. They zip by the crowd at over 200 miles per hour. The Indy 500, as it is known, is held in Indianapolis on the last Sunday in May.

Bill Monroe Bluegrass Festival

Banjo players, fiddlers, and singers gather at Bean Blossom in June to share their love of bluegrass music. Bill Monroe, who is known as the father of bluegrass, founded the festival in 1967.

The Indy 500

Madison Regatta

The town of Madison has seen plenty of river traffic pass on the Ohio. In July, high-powered hydroplanes speed by in the Madison Regatta and the Governor's Cup race.

Indiana State Fair

Indiana farmers show their best livestock and farm products and manufacturers display the latest farm equipment and methods at the State Fair. The fair is held in August in Indianapolis. The first fair was held in 1852.

Grabill Country Fair

Traditional crafts and food draw people to the town of Grabill in September, on the weekend after Labor Day. Music and contests for children and adults add to the festivities.

Riley Festival

The October birthday of Indiana poet James Whitcomb Riley is celebrated in Greenfield, which is Riley's birthplace. The Parade of Flowers, in which children leave flowers at the statue of Riley, is a tradition of the festival.

A colonial festival in Lafayette

4 How It Works

Indiana has had two state constitutions. The first one was written in 1816, a little before Indiana became a state. The second constitution was written in 1851 and is the present-day constitution. The Indiana constitution begins with a bill of rights, which is a list of basic rights guaranteed to each person. The constitution also describes the organization of the state government.

The State Capitol in Indianapolis.

Counties, Cities, Towns, and Townships

The state of Indiana is divided into ninety-two counties. Counties are made up of cities, towns, and townships. The state's legislature, also called the General Assembly, decides how the county and city governments are to be organized. These rules are spelled out in the Indiana Code. According to the Code, counties, cities, towns, and townships are governed by a legislative branch and an executive branch. The counties, cities, towns, and townships have what is called home rule. This means that they may create rules and may form committees and agencies as needed. It allows them to conduct business in their areas for the good of their residents.

In Indiana's counties, boards of commissioners are the executive branch, while a county council serves as the legislative body. Each city has a mayor as its executive and a common council as the legislative body. The legislative body in a town is the town council. The president of the town council is the town's executive. A township is led by a trustee and a township board. People are elected from their own county, city, town, or township to serve in these jobs.

The government of the city of Indianapolis and Marion County is different from that is the other cities in Indiana. In 1970, Indianapolis became what is called a consolidated city. The boundaries of Indianapolis were extended to match the boundaries of Marion County, in which Indianapolis is located. In addition, the branches of the city and the county governments were combined to form a new government called Unigov. Unigov has three branches. The legislative body is the city-county council. The mayor and the mayor's office form

Branches of Government

Executive The governor is Indiana's chief executive. The governor and lieutenant governor are elected together to serve for four years. The other elected officials in the executive branch are the attorney general, secretary of state, auditor, treasurer, superintendent of public instruction, and clerk of courts. The executive branch enforces the laws of Indiana.

Legislative The state legislature is known as the General Assembly. It has two houses, the senate and the house of representatives. The senate has fifty members and the house of representatives has one hundred members. Senators are elected to a four-year term and representatives to a two-year term. In odd-numbered years, the General Assembly meets in a sixty-one day session. In even-numbered years, it meets for thirty days. The General Assembly creates laws for the state.

Judicial The supreme court is the highest court in Indiana. It has five justices, one of whom is the chief justice. The state has five courts of appeal, each with three justices. The supreme court and the courts of appeal review the decisions made in the lower courts. Trials are conducted by the circuit courts. Some counties have superior courts and juvenile courts. There are also county, city, and municipal courts.

the executive branch. A circuit court, superior court, and small claims court form the judicial branch.

State Government

Like the federal government, the Indiana government has three branches. These three branches are the executive, the legislative, and the judicial. Each branch has its own powers and responsibilities. The executive branch is headed by the governor. The legislative branch is the lawmaking body. The judicial branch consists of the courts.

The people of Indiana are also represented in the United States Congress in Washington, D.C. Indiana elects nine representatives to the U.S. House of Representatives and two senators to the United States Senate. Every four years, Hoosiers cast their ballots for president.

How a Bill Becomes a Law

Indiana's legislators create laws and programs to help their districts and the state. For example, they vote on the amount of money to spend on programs such as education, transportation, and public health.

In the legislative process, a law begins as a bill, which is a proposal, or suggestion, for a law. To reach its final form, a bill goes through a series of steps. If a bill is to become a law, it must be kept alive all through the process. At any stage, if it does not advance to the next step, the bill may die.

Any senator or representative may introduce a bill. Often the ideas for bills comes from state residents. Once a bill is introduced, it then travels through its house of origin, either the senate or the house of representatives.

After the bill is introduced it is scheduled for its first reading. At the first reading, the title is read aloud to the legislators. Then the bill is assigned to a committee of legislators. The committee schedules a public hearing for the bill. Anyone may come to the hearing to discuss the things they like and the things they do not like about the bill. After the hearing, the committee may vote on the bill or table it. If the committee tables the bill, it will die unless the committee votes on it later. In the vote, the committee decides whether to advance the bill or to let it die.

If the bill advances, it is eligible for a second reading. At the second reading, legislators may propose amendments or changes to the bill. For an amendment to be added, it must be approved by a majority of the legislators. Then the bill is voted on.

The bill is now ready for the third reading. If a third reading is scheduled, more amendments can be proposed. For these amendments to be added, they must be approved by a two-thirds majority of the legislators. This means that two-thirds of the legislators must vote in favor of the amendments. Then the bill is voted on again. If enough legislators vote in favor of the bill, it will move on to the next house— either the senate of the house of representatives.

If the bill makes it through both the senate and the house of representatives, then it goes to the governor. When presented with a bill, the governor has three choices. The

State legislators work inside the State Capitol. These are the House Chambers, where the state representatives meet.

governor can sign the bill into law or can do nothing, and the bill will become a law anyway. The governor can also veto or reject the bill. The legislators, however, can try to override the veto. A majority of both the senators and the representatives is required to override the governor's veto and to make the bill a law.

Getting Involved

Voters stay informed so they can understand the different sides of issues and can pick candidates who share their ideas and principles. They listen to television and radio reports, read the papers, and talk with their neighbors. Many people attend the public meetings of the state and local governments. Hoosiers contribute to the decision-making process of their state by writing to their legislators and speaking at hearings. They organize campaigns and volunteer their time to create interest and support for their favorite issues and candidates. Students who are curious about the workings of the General Assembly can serve as a senate page for a day.

To find Indiana's legislative districts and the state and federal legislators, go to this Web site www.in.gov/apps/sos/legislator/search/ Fill in your ZIP code, or click on the link, for the state map. When the map appears, click on your county to find your district and representatives.

5 Making a Living

Indiana has a reputation for being an agricultural state. People working in agriculture make a significant contribution to the economy, yet other activities contribute to the state economy as well. People work in manufacturing, service jobs, transportation, and mining, too. In Indiana, the proportion of the workforce working in manufacturing is greater than that in any other state.

Agriculture Today

Farms are found throughout Indiana, especially in the northern two thirds of the state. Even urban counties, like Marion and Lake Counties, have some farmland. The soil, rainfall, and hot summers of Indiana make its farmland very productive.

Of all the agricultural products, corn brings in the most income. Soybeans are second, and hogs are third. Much of the corn, soybean, and oat harvests are used as animal feed for

Farmer's markets set up on Indiana's city streets are a blend of the old and new. Agriculture has long been an important part of Indiana's economy, but the industry has had to adapt to changing times.

Indiana's hogs and other livestock. Corn is also sold as fresh ears, and some is packaged as popcorn.

"Indiana has the best tomatoes," claims one Hoosier. Indiana grows tomatoes for eating fresh and for processing. Cantaloupes and watermelons grow in the sandy soil of southwestern Indiana. Winter wheat, potatoes, hay, cucumbers for pickles, green beans, tobacco, and onions are also important crops. Fruits include apples, peaches, and blueberries.

Poultry farms raise chickens, ducks, and turkeys. Some poultry farms specialize in egg and baby chick production. Ice cream is a leading dairy product. Indiana's meat packing industry processes hogs, cattle, sheep, and poultry.

A hog farm near Brownsburg.

Recipe for Mint-Chocolate Brownies

Mint is an important Indiana product. Following this recipe, you can make a batch of brownies with a refreshing minty flavor.

Ingredients:

3/4 cups butter	3 eggs
1-1/2 cups sugar	1/2 cup cocoa powder
1 teaspoon of vanilla	3/4 cups flour
1/2 teaspoon of mint flavoring	1/2 teaspoon baking powder

Have an adult help you with the oven. Preheat the oven to 350 degrees. Grease a brownie pan with a little bit of oil and set the pan to the side.

Put the butter in a mixing bowl and beat it until it is fluffy. Add the eggs, sugar, vanilla, and mint flavorings. Make sure all the ingredients are mixed very well.

Add the cocoa, flour, baking powder, and just a pinch of salt and continue mixing until the batter is smooth. Carefully pour the batter into the pan.

Place the pan in the middle of the rack in the oven. Bake your brownies for about 30 minutes. You can check if they are done by carefully sticking a knife or a toothpick into the center of the pan. If the brownies are done, the knife or toothpick will come out clean. You can ask an adult to help you with this.

When the brownies are done baking, carefully take them out of the oven and set them aside to cool. When they are cool you can cut them into small squares. Serve the brownies plain or with a little bit of ice cream or whipped cream.

Products & Resources

Mint

Peppermint and spearmint are grown in northwestern Indiana for their flavorful oil. In summer, the tops of the leafy plants are harvested and the oil is distilled from them. Peppermint and spearmint oils are added to chewing gum, toothpaste, mouthwash, candy, and medicines.

Band Instruments

Trumpets, trombones, flutes, piccolos, clarinets, oboes, bassoons, saxophones, tubas, and sousaphones are among the band instruments manufactured in Indiana. Skilled musicians as well as beginners play these brass and woodwind instruments.

Furniture and Cabinets

Indiana is a top producer of wood office furniture and kitchen cabinets. Oak, maple, tulip tree, ash, hickory, and cherry are favorite choices. These beautiful woods come from the forests of Indiana and neighboring states.

Orthopedic Implants

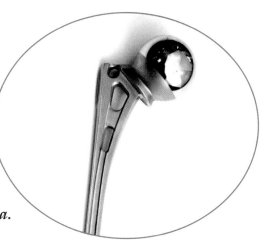

Artificial knees, hips, shoulders, elbows, and ankles are designed to replace diseased or damaged joints in people. Some companies that make orthopedic implants are centered in Warsaw, Indiana.

Soybeans

Soybeans grown in Indiana feed the state's hogs and other livestock. The nutritious beans and oil are also added to many food products sold in the grocery store. Soybean oil has nonfood uses, too. It is made into ink, crayons, and candles. Biodiesel fuel—which contains soybean oil—powers trucks, tractors, and buses.

Recreational Vehicles

Many campers, trailers, motor homes, and recreational vehicles (RVs) are made in Indiana. Some manufacturers build the shell of these vehicles while others craft and install all the interior details.

Manufacturing

Indiana's factories make and process a great range of products. The Calumet region of northwest Indiana is known for the production of high quality steel. To make the steel, ingredients such as iron, coke, and limestone are heated in blast furnaces. The coke is made in the Calumet region, too. It is made from coal that is baked until it is almost pure carbon. At mini-mills, scrap steel is melted so it can be re-used. Steel beams, household and medical appliances, machinery, cans, and motor vehicles and parts are only a few of the things made of steel.

Indiana is a leader in the production of auto parts. Its factories turn out brakes, axles, pistons, exhaust pipes, carburetors, lighting, and electrical components for cars and trucks. There are

Workers assemble car parts at an automotive factory in Greencastle.

also companies that make diesel engines for buses and heavy-duty construction equipment. Some plants make the bodies for delivery vans, trucks, ambulances, and shuttle buses. Other plants assemble cars and trucks. Campers, RVs, and motor homes are a specialty in Indiana's motor vehicle industry.

Major pharmaceutical companies have production plants and laboratories in Indiana. They research new drugs and treatments for both humans and animals and make pills and medicines. The pharmaceutical

Drug research and manufacturing in Indiana has created many medicines that have helped people across the country and around the world.

company Eli Lilly and Company is the largest single employer in Indiana. The company has a history of medical breakthroughs. It was the first to sell insulin as a treatment for diabetes, and it develops many other important drugs.

Indiana's forests supply the forest products and hardwood industries. Loggers harvest the trees, and at sawmills, the logs are cut into boards. The wood is used in house construction and to make furniture. Trees such as cherry and walnut are cut into thin layers of veneer. Veneer is used to cover furniture to give it beauty. Pulp made from scraps and odd pieces of wood is turned into paper products. Each step of the manufacturing process adds value to the wood and creates jobs.

Unfortunately, in recent years, a number of Indiana factories have closed. In many cases the factory was an important part of the community. The loss of the factory is often troublesome to a town and a hardship for the people who once worked there. When the company ArvinMeritor closed its factory in Franklin, the town's clerk-treasurer Janet Alexander said, "It's hard to imagine the community without them. They've been a source of pride for the community for as long as I can remember." When this happens, many workers either move to other cities and states in search of jobs or learn a new trade.

Mining

Limestone may be the most widely known mineral of Indiana. The light gray or light tan stone covers many important buildings in the state and in the nation. Limestone is also carved into statues and into building elements such as columns and decorative molding. Limestone is cut from quarries in south-central Indiana. Coal is taken from strip mines in southwestern Indiana. Sand, gravel, clay, and shale are also widely collected. Limestone, sand, shale, and iron oxide are combined to make cement. Indiana also produces oil and natural gas.

Transportation

Highways, railroads, airports, marine ports help Indiana's farmers and manufacturers to reach their customers. These passageways connect Indiana's cities and towns with Chicago, Illinois, and Louisville, Kentucky, and other transportation hubs throughout the nation. Trucks travel the

The mining industry provides jobs for Indiana residents.

interstate highways across northern and southern Indiana and north and south through Indianapolis. Railroads converge on Indianapolis, too. Indiana has three ports, two on the Ohio River and one on Lake Michigan. These ports receive large shipments of grain, coal, steel, and fertilizer. Ships leave these ports and travel all the way to the Atlantic Ocean and the Gulf of Mexico.

Highways not only help people get to and from work and to find relaxing recreation areas, they also attract businesses and jobs to the areas they pass through. A number

This ship is being used to transport iron ore from Gary.

of high-technology companies are situated along Interstate 65, near West Lafayette and Purdue University, and along Interstate 69 in northeastern Indiana. Plans are underway to extend Interstate 69 from Indianapolis to Evansville in the southwest. People hope that the new highway will draw new companies and people to southern Indiana and give the state economy a boost.

Service

Service jobs involve practicing a special skill or helping another individual or business. Tourism in Indiana is a service industry. The people who work in hotels, restaurants,

People who work in stores and markets are a part of the widespread service industry in Indiana.

and stores are all considered service workers. Also included are museum workers, and tour guides.

Service workers also provide dental care, business management, and legal advice. They perform jobs such as sales, computer programming, and accounting. They make car repairs and do cleaning. Counselors, teachers, and scientists are counted as service workers. In Indiana, health care workers, businesspeople, office workers, and foodservice workers are the most numerous representatives of this category.

The people of Indiana work together so that the products they make and the services they provide are the best in the world. They have used the resources of their state to make it a leader in agriculture and in manufacturing. They continue to invent modern and useful products that are used throughout the nation and the world. People who work in transportation try new ways to move goods through the state as quickly and efficiently as possible. They help Indiana to send its products to far away places. More and more, scientists and businesspeople in Indiana work together. They combine their ideas and knowledge and think of new ways to create products that will improve health care and agriculture. The energy and creativity of the people of Indiana have helped to give the state a strong economy. Indianans make their state a good place to work and to live.

The torch at the center of the Indiana flag stands for liberty and enlightenment. The rays coming from the flame represent their far-reaching effect. Thirteen stars are arranged in a circle around the torch. They represent the original thirteen states. The five stars arranged in a half-circle represent the next five states to be admitted to the Union. The large star above the torch represents the nineteenth state, Indiana.

The state seal is in the shape of a circle. The outer circular band bears the words "Seal of the State of Indiana." The date 1816 is the year that Indiana became a state. The small design on either side of the date includes the leaf of the tulip tree, the state tree. The inner circle has two sycamore trees at the right. A man raises an ax to swing at the trees. On the left, a buffalo jumps over a log and into green grass. In the background, the sun shines above three hills.

INDIANA

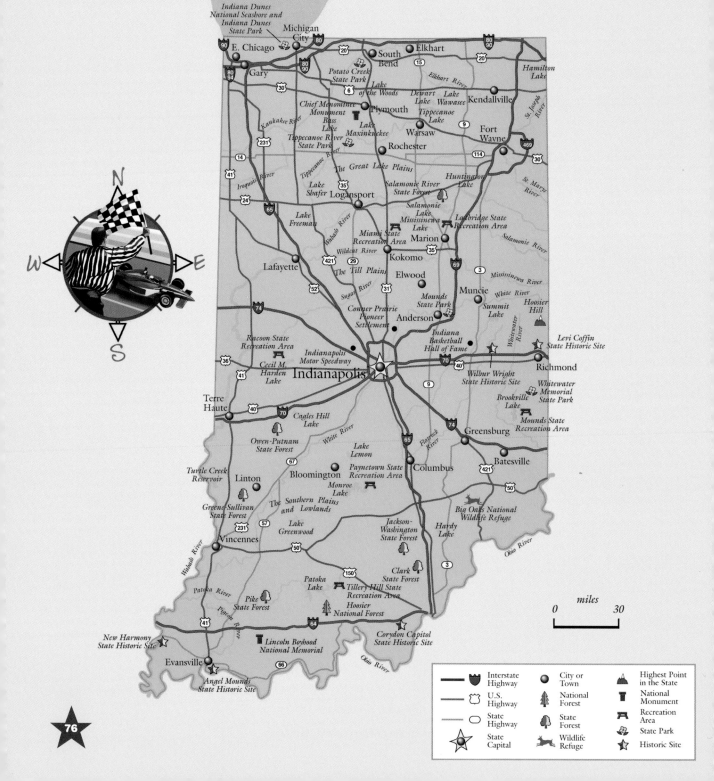

LAKE
MICHIGAN

Indiana Dunes
National Seashore and
Indiana Dunes
State Park

Michigan
City

90 E. Chicago

80
94 Gary

South
Bend

Elkhart

Hamilton
Lake

Potato Creek
State Park

Elkhart River

Lake
of the Woods

30

Chief Menominee
Monument
Bass
Lake

Plymouth

Dewart Lake
Lake Wawasee

Kendallville

St. Joseph River

Kankakee River

231

Lake
Maxinkuckee

Tippecanoe
Lake

Warsaw

Fort
Wayne

469

Tippecanoe River
State Park

Rochester

114

14

41

Tippecanoe River

The Great Lake Plains

Huntington
Lake

30

Iroquois River

Lake
Shafer

Salamonie River
State Forest

St. Marys
River

24

35

Logansport

Salamonie
Lake

Salamonie River

65

Lake
Freeman

Wabash River

Mississinewa
Lake

Lostbridge State
Recreation Area

Miami State
Recreation Area

Marion

Lafayette

421

Wildcat River

Kokomo

35

3

Mississinewa River

52

29

The Till Plains

Sugar River

31

Elwood

Muncie

White River

Summit
Lake

Hoosier
Hill

74

Conner Prairie
Pioneer
Settlement

Mounds
State Park

Anderson

69

Racoon State
Recreation Area

Indiana
Basketball
Hall of Fame

Levi Coffin
State Historic Site

36

Cecil M.
Harden Lake

Indianapolis
Motor Speedway

70

40

Wilbur Wright
State Historic Site

Richmond

41

Indianapolis

9

Whitewater
Memorial
State Park

Terre
Haute

40

Brookville
Lake

70

Cagles Hill
Lake

White River

65

Flatrock River

74

Greensburg

Mounds State
Recreation Area

Owen-Putnam
State Forest

67

Lake
Lemon

Paynetown State
Recreation Area

Columbus

421

Batesville

50

Turtle Creek
Reservoir

Linton

Bloomington

Monroe
Lake

Big Oaks National
Wildlife Refuge

Greene-Sullivan
State Forest

231

57

Lake
Greenwood

Jackson-
Washington
State Forest

Hardy
Lake

3

Vincennes

50

150

Ohio River

Wabash River

Patoka River

Patoka
Lake

Clark
State
Forest

Tillery Hill State
Recreation Area

Pigeon River

Pike
State Forest

Hoosier
National Forest

41

64

Corydon Capitol
State Historic Site

New Harmony
State Historic Site

Lincoln Boyhood
National Memorial

Evansville

66

Ohio River

Angel Mounds
State Historic Site

miles
0   30

★ 76

Interstate Highway	City or Town		Highest Point in the State	
U.S. Highway	National Forest		National Monument	
State Highway	State Forest		Recreation Area	
State Capital	Wildlife Refuge		State Park	
			Historic Site	

On the Banks of the Wabash, Far Away

Words and music by Paul Dresser

State Song

More About Indiana

Books

Brunelle, Lynn. *Indiana, The Hoosier State.* Milwaukee, WI: World Almanac Library, 2002.

Johnson, Oliver. *A Home in the Woods: Oliver Johnson's Reminiscences of Early Marion County as Related by Howard Johnson.* Bloomington and Indianapolis: Indiana University Press, 1978.

Ross, D.J. *Uniquely Indiana.* Chicago: Heinemann Library, 2004.

Stratton-Porter, Gene. *Laddie: A True Blue Story.* Wheaton, IL: Tyndale House Publishers, 1991.

Web Sites

State of Indiana Official Web Site
http://www.state.in.us

Indiana Dunes National Lakeshore
http://www.nps.gov/indu

Indiana Official Tourism Site
http://www.enjoyindiana.com

About the Author

Kathleen Derzipilski is a research editor who specializes in children's nonfiction. She lives in San Diego, California.

Index

Page numbers in **boldface** are illustrations.